Dalisay

Written by Casey Tainter

Copyright © 2017 by Casey Tainter
All rights reserved. This book or any portion thereof may not be reproduced or used in any manner without the prior written consent from the author.

Publication, Editorial, and Design by Sonder R. Publishing
www.SonderRPublishing.com

Printed in the United States of America
ISBN: 978-0-692913-14-7

Cover Photo by Tanya Ostapyuk
www.tanyaost.com

Dedicated to loved ones.

The ones who are with us and ones who are not -

- Contents -

Her

Imprint 3	Lucy 29
The Power in Poetry 5	Others Who? 31
Surrender 7	Blind 33
Darla 9	Georgiana 35
Hello 11	M & M 37
Get it Together 13	Huntress 39
Ballerina 15	Drift 41
Unknown Friend 17	Welcome Home 43
San Francisco 19	California 45
Tanya 21	I Met Alice 47
Riverwalk 23	Beauty 49
Aimee 25	Cheers 51
A Poets Emotions 27	

Love

He Is My Favorite Poem 55	Rush of Lust 87
Catch & Release 57	Exceptional 89
Wild One 59	Imbroglio 91
Wallet Photo 61	Dreaming of You 93
Quit You 63	Wholesome 95
Erased 65	Presence 97
Repentance 67	Liaison 99
Superman 69	Lost Cowboys 101
Escape 71	Tiny Fairies 103
Hello Again 73	Dalliance 105
Stay 75	Should Have Seen This Coming ... 107
Say Love 77	Lascivious 109
Take Me Back to Earth 79	Ghost 111
Finding You 81	Insulin 113
Lesson Number One 83	His Promise 115
Suspension 85	

Heartbreak

- Vacancy ... 119
- More Than Words ... 121
- Unlabeled File Cabinet ... 123
- I Don't Need You ... 125
- Remember My Name ... 127
- Cruel Thoughts ... 129
- Diabolical ... 131
- Grounded by You ... 133
- Leaving ... 135
- Vs. ... 137
- Don't Know Me Anymore ... 139
- Surviving His Lies ... 141
- Your Message Has Been Sent ... 143
- Puzzle Piece ... 145
- Goodbye Lonely ... 147
- Inferno ... 149
- Onions & Men ... 151
- Numb ... 153
- 6.5 ... 155
- Home Invasion ... 157
- Slipping into Absence ... 159
- In the Reserve ... 161
- Days in Counting ... 163
- You Don't Love Me ... 165
- Knotted ... 167
- Hollow ... 169

Dénouement

- Tribute ... 173
- Old Soul ... 175
- Begging Tumble Weed ... 177
- Don't Blink ... 179
- Lioness ... 181
- Analyzing the World ... 183
- I Don't Drink ... 185
- A Desert Dream ... 187
- Little Feet ... 189
- Monday's ... 191

About ... 193

Her

Her love
Her heartbreak
Her dénouement -

Dalisay

Imprint

I bet you wonder if you're in it
Is there a mention of all your monsters?

There might be.

But then again,
Maybe that one poem you thought was about you,
   wasn't about you.

Maybe you've faded from my memory,
Forever lost to an occurrence in time.

But that's your deepest fear, isn't it?
Not of what you'll read about yourself,

But what you may not find.

Dalisay

The Power in Poetry

She let her words flow like the quickest stream
Falling from the glaciers to the meadow -
Her mind never rests,
So full of life
Healing the valley's drought

Her waters are soothing,
The resonance of rhythm
The sound of silence

Her words will baptize you
Make you believe in another power,
The strength in solitude
The power in poetry.

Surrender

I'm feeling in tune with myself
Hand me a pen
Let it write away my deepest apologies
And confess all my sins

Let this black ink stir rhythm
And sing to your soul
Dropping you to your knees
Forfeiting your control

It's curving and twisting
All around this notepad
Telling you things about myself
That I never would have said.

Darla

The innocence that remains inside of me
Darla, is what her name shall be.

Running through the forest as if she were free
Wearing a vintage white dress
With scrapes on her knees
The lightest shade of blonde hair that you ever did see
Dirt on her hands while her supper seat remains empty.

Darla, oh Darla, where might you be?
Chasing the butterflies and buzzing with the bees
Napping in the meadow and jumping from trees.

Dreaming of Darla, she and I are dancing
Away with each other, where I wish I could be her
And she wishes she were me.

Hello

Hello poetry -
Have you come to whisk me away into another fantasy
Float me down the river of another memory
Guide me into an abyss, searching for my sanity
Remove me from this place, drifting from gravity

I shut my eyes and let poetry do away with me.

Dalisay

Get it Together

I'm out of my right mind sometimes
Good thing I have my left side to fall back on -

Ballerina

She dances
Alone
In such grace and poise
Positioned in between the tallest buildings
She poses
For the camera
For the blinding flashes.

She dances
On stage
In the spotlight
Twirling and twisting
Not a hair out of place
Not a step out of line
Not a breath unplanned.

Trained to be accurate
Self destructing, but so well collected
The most beautiful dancer the world has ever seen.

Dalisay

Unknown Friend

I read your poems and I feel as if I know you
As if I have known you for your entire life
As if I have witnessed every smile and tear in the night
Every nightmare that causes you fright
I read your poems and I feel as if I know you.

I read your poems and I feel like you trust me
Like I am your dearest friend and you confide only in me
So close we are, you confess everything
I read your poems and I feel like you trust me.

I read your poems in silence and forget where I am
Line after line, I nod my head because I understand
I read about you and where it all began
I put you down then pick you up, and am lost once again.

San Francisco

I left my heart in San Francisco
I lost my mind in Alcatraz
Atop the waves of the bay that day
I realized I could never go back.

I realized all decisions were final
And to be in love is a fatal thing
That sometimes you see the best in someone,
Even when there is no good to be seen.

The busy city streets that whistle
Screaming life and revealing 'self'
Could make a person feel the most whole or empty
Depending on which corner you find yourself.

On that island that caged so many
Who could hear life from out of view
Left behind a shallowness and cruelty
That somehow reminded me of you.

Tanya

Write about me, she said
Write me a poem and tell it to the stars
Talk about my hidden talents
Or confess my many scars.

But her beauty could not be captured
By any photo or ball point pen
And no length of poetic summaries could ever
Express the fire that she holds within.

Even Venus, she is envious of her
As she walks this earth with grace
A fallen angel from the heavens above
To know her soul is to know real strength.

She twirls her arms above her head
As she dances down the street
Twisting and turning away with the wind
With the prettiest smile you ever did see.

She needs nothing from you, and she takes nothing more
She comes and goes softly with poise
With all the beauty she possesses she is still
  so compassionate
Because that is who she is, by choice.

Dalisay

Riverwalk

I walked as far as I could
Off the beaten path
Between the weeds and overgrowth,

Next to the river
I found a fountain
I found a spot that felt like home.

I stayed just to listen
To feel my heart beat once again
I forgot what it was like to feel alive,

I don't know how to be me
Or, more like me
The girl I know is trapped inside.

Aimee

I crawled off the Muni
Gagging from too much liquor
Smeared ash from the ground on my face
Sitting next to the Quick Stop, with a left over Miller

I waited for you, Aimee
I've been waiting for someone like you
Innocence that should surround you
Somberly painted in hues

The roaring of armed pedestrians
A home made of paper and broken glass
You sat next to me for someone to listen
And I was going nowhere fast

I listened and I heard your pain
Too young to know it's not normal
Sweet thing, don't give up
Resist the inevitable,

These people will dye your skin new colors
And time will show you no mercy
I've waited a lifetime for you to be here with me today
For someone to listen to this advice,
  that I wish someone would have given me.

A Poets Emotions

We feel so deep that we reach an abyss
We feel nothing when we feel everything all at once
Our hearts are trying to send too much data to our brains

O v e r l o a d !

Lucy

Shoot me up, just a taste
Numb my core with sweet Novocain
Poison my veins, rippling clear across my brain
So strong that I don't feel a single thing
Not a pinch of delight, veering on the edge of insane
In a dream-like state
Soundlessly floating away -

I've met you before, Lucy
But this time I intend to stay
I'm captivated by your prison,
Chained inside your domain
In this realm of impurity,
You are my sole desired escape.

Others Who?

Do you mean the ones who live on the other side?
Clear across the ocean, two miles in from the tide?

The ones that live with little means,
Or the ones that live like we were meant to?
That work, play, stress, fear, and cry, just like we do?

The men who were created from the earth
And the women from Adams rib?
The ones who fall asleep staring at the same galaxies
Wondering if we're all there is?

Do you mean the ones in straw houses off dirt roads?
That learn how to survive on the land
And wear the clothes that they sew?

Others and me, I'm sorry pardon me,
I'm just slightly confused
Because when I think of them, I think of me
I can't separate the two.

Blind

What if we could read another person's thoughts?
What if we could hear their mind?
If we could see what they think
We may be better off blind.

Georgiana

I saw her
In the dark, in that alley way
Leaned against the wall
One foot resting behind her,
One slightly in front.

She smoked her cigarette and looked at me
Like I didn't know about pain.

She hardly saw me
But I saw her every night
I passed her and she always waited
For the next guest, for the next moment.

She was like chalk
Pale and stale, diminishing and broken
I noted her dark red lipstick
Compared against her white skin and black hair
It was the closest thing to life that I could relate her to.

Her eyes would follow my footsteps past her
I watched her contemplate her choices
As I faded down the misty street
But still every night, I continued to see her.

Dalisay

M & M

Mustard & Mayonnaise sandwiches
Because nobody grocery shops in this place
After some time I learned to adapt
And it just became the new way.

Oversleeping through breakfast
Lunch is noon and night
Mustard & Mayonnaise sandwiches
Because they satisfy my appetite.

I begged my dad for turkey and swiss
But he always managed to forget
And when friends asked "what do you got to eat"?
I'd reply "Mustard & Mayonnaise sandwiches".

It's the little things we remember when we grow up
The dullest things can be so significant
They're a symbol of my childhood,
Those Mustard & Mayonnaise sandwiches.

Dalisay

Huntress

She was the fighter, the rebel
Hidden behind cherry lips
Pale and slender, a voice that would make you surrender
With eyes like an eclipse.

Carefully plotted schemes she carried
Delicate steps she always took
Armed with an army of mischievous intentions
She played the role of a good girl, but she was
  undoubtedly a crook.

Ask any man, he'll tell you so
She had a reputation like no other
If you'd met her, you'd surely wish you hadn't
They call her the Heart Hunter.

Dalisay

Drift

From my three-story apartment window,
I hear the 2am bar fights.

I overhear the sirens of the city race by
The breaking glass from another nomad
Tangled with the sound of drunken couples,
Who hate each other as they stumble,
Pushing through the murky alley below me,
Passing the muffled moans of infidelities -

I feel the breeze blended with artists' dreams pass by
I lay in this Cal. King drowning in pillows,
Staring at these passé stained white walls that have been
  molested by so many forgotten visitors
I lay here and I know why I lay alone.

I'm so consumed by the life outside my window
That I do not notice when a life walks out my front door.

Welcome Home

Welcome home to reality where you lose what you love
This place you call safe, may not be secure enough.

This land you call free may leave you broken and bare
And just when you think you've made it,
You're nowhere near there.

Welcome home to this place that is fueled
  by power and greed
Give it your best shot, but you may never succeed.

Hope for the best but you may shatter your dreams
You can cling to hold it together while falling apart
  at the seams.

California

She is the crisp air that fills my lungs
The damp salty wind in my beach hair
The cold wet sand between my toes
My young blood on these city streets.

From the snowflakes on my tongue
To the redwoods that surround me
Her independence and diversity
Are my sweetest comfort.

As I drive south with her at my back
It is a sad and painful goodbye.

Dalisay

I Met Alice

I tripped down an endless rabbit hole
Some might say I was swallowed
I fell down, down, and tumbled around
Until I forgot the land of tomorrow.

I met Alice and she was darling
We sipped tea and spoke of rhymes
Trying to decode the words of the Hatter
Searching for where the rabbit lost his time.

We danced on the shore of day and night
Followed paths until they were swept away
And when we were tired and had enough
We snuck into court and extended our stay.

Alice and I, oh how we fell
Off the earth and into abyss
Absorbed by each other, forgetting our troubles
Spending each remaining day in complete bliss.

Dalisay

Beauty

You relinquish your beauty when you allow others to decide what is beautiful about you.

Cheers

Maybe one day I'll finish these half-started rhymes
When the day comes where I can lay in tulips all day
Sipping a bottle of wine
When the earth stops spinning and I'm resting on cloud -

So here's to another half-finished piece
Maybe it'll find you more solace than it ever did me.

Love

The most painful comfort we continue to crave

Dalisay

He Is My Favorite Poem

When I think of you, I think of poetry
I think of my favorite words
Ever so carefully written
Methodically planned in rhythm
Like lyrics I can't forget,
When they seep into my soul
And smear ink all over my mind.

Dalisay

Catch & Release

His arms held me so tight that I could not escape
His kisses kidnapped me
His smile captured my heart.

But he freed me,
And that is what made me solely his.

Dalisay

Wild One

There was something wild in her
Something corrupt
Something destructive.

I often wondered if there was a fighter plane
Soaring high in her skies
Fighting to defend something precious.

There was something wild in her
Something loud
Something overwhelming.

I observed her in her calmest state and watched
  as she demanded power from others
But in the most manipulative way,
Where you would never know it was a command.

There was something wild in her
Something loving
Something passionate.

I was blessed to lay with her from time to time
I wanted her heart for all of these reasons,
But she was too wild for anyone.

Dalisay.

Wallet Photo

He keeps her photo in his wallet
From all those years back when
They made mistakes and loved each other
In those brief summer months spent

He keeps her photo there for certainty -
To remind him that love is real
And even though he threw it all away with her,
The picture helps him heal

So many years have passed since then
And she was so long ago
She still looks just the way as he remembers her
When pulls out that old wallet photo.

Dalisay

Quit You

I was the sweet sugar on his mouth
Melted on his tongue
Like snowflakes
Tingling his senses
A refreshing experience
And he sipped me like coffee
Like some kind of caffeine addict -
Again and again pressed against his lips
I wanted so much to be his habit
Oh but I was, and I'll never forget it
He's long gone now
And I'm just that stained mug in his cabinet.

Dalisay

Erased

I began to write this about him
But as I started,
His face disappeared and all I could think about was you.

Within seconds my heartbreak and brokenness
Was suddenly and entirely *gone -*

Dalisay

Repentance

I traded in my crucifix to run away with a man
The life of a rebel,
My life with a criminal -
Battling my conscience with the devil.

Second guessing & rethinking my ways
Freedom tastes so sweet
But is the price worth the pay?
My skin burns as my religion renounces me,

Yet my heart beats to his drum
Sins and all
Loving him is a guilty liberation
A brutal descent, a satisfying fall.

Dalisay

Superman

He grabbed her hand
  Covered her eyes
    Snatched her from gravity
      Flew her to the highest point in the skies
        Held her body tight

"O p e n   y o u r   e y e s"

She did and what she saw was terrifying
  The world beneath her feet

He said
  Don't be scared
    I've got you
      And I'm *never* letting you go.

Escape

If for a moment she could escape, she would
Even if just for a few hours
Lost in silence or lost in a crowd.

She chose to escape in him.

And had she known
That was the most dangerous thing she could have done,
I believe she still would have done it all the same.

Dalisay

Hello Again

Somewhere in the shadows I found you.
I don't recall what I was searching for
I don't remember how I got there
But I recollect the overwhelming warmth of finally feeling
  complete when my eyes happened upon you.
When I close my eyes I can still see your light brown eyes
  find mine for the first time.

In that moment, we were one
For a second, you were mine and I was yours.

Stay

You make me feel like I've been waiting for you
    for a lifetime.

Dalisay

Say Love

You speak of love as if you should know it
But you have never fallen in love with a poet

You have never been captivated by a sentence or a phrase
A heartfelt tribute that would leave you weakened
  for days

You have never been held prisoner by a verse about love
A single idea expressed in rhythm that would make you
  feel like you could never get enough

You've never read an emotion that broke your heart and
  broke you down
No, you've never loved so deep that you thought you
  might drown

I love you this way, the same that I love my lyrics
If you can feel what I feel, then tell me so I can hear it.

Take Me Back to Earth

Please put me down

I let you take me above and beyond
Soaring through the galaxies

You've shown me the brightest stars
  and the kindest planets
You've shown me compassion in ways
  I've never known
You've shown me honesty and love -

But please put me down,
  and bring me back to Earth.

I don't want to fall from all the way up here
I don't want to be abandoned out here

Please bring me back,
Where I know what to expect.
And even though it's less than what I deserve,
At least I will know where I stand.

Dalisay

Finding You

In the middle of a dead field
Nowhere to be
Yellow mountains and abandoned dirt roads
Surround me

Thoughts of you keep me moving
I'd follow you with bare feet
Across California until my hands find yours again
You are the half that completes me

Free to make a choice
Free to give my heart away
No matter how far you go,
To you I will always find a way.

Dalisay

Lesson Number One

You felt something strong
Something powerful, overbearing
And it consumed you
But it was not love.

You felt something real and unimaginable
Something that could not be put into words
Nor stopped by the grace of God
But it was not love.

You felt touched by another's soul
And suffocated under his sweet words
Forceful hands that made you scream into a pillow
Left you breathless and dazed
But it was not love.

You felt passion and lust for the first time, my dear
But it was not love.

Dalisay

Suspension

My universe comes to an unnerving halt
  when I see you -

But I continue to walk,
  as if I'm in a rush with somewhere to be.

Rush of Lust

I was swept off my feet
When you grabbed me by the arm
You stole me away into the night
And had me completely disarmed.

I couldn't see anything around
Except tall buildings and fainted lights
We ran through alley ways
Up and down stairs, we took flight.

My hand in your hand
Your eyes spoke in rhythm to me
Your kisses and your fingers
All over my body.

Tonight, you will have me
And tomorrow I'll be gone
Just as quickly as we met
We both will have moved on.

Dalisay

Exceptional

Out of all the subjects of love my dear,
You are by far my favorite.

Imbroglio

He offered her the world
She said she only desired his heart
He paused for a moment with a look of confusion
As he did not know where to start.

Dreaming of You

I've been dreaming lately
Painting watercolor images on the canvas in my mind
Watching romantic movies on my eyelids
Singing in my sleep.

I wake up whispering "I love you"
Sometimes your forehead is resting on mine as I say it
Other times you're walking away -
The scenario continues to change,
But the result is always the same
I continue to love you.

Dalisay

Wholesome

If I know of but only one thing to be true,
It is that I am more myself when I am with you.

Dalisay

Presence

I don't mean to love you
It just is this way,

And I've tried everything
Literally, everything
To let go of you

Yet you always stay.

Liaison

I thought that maybe if I was his secret,
He would keep me forever.

Lost Cowboys

Those brothers were Cowboys
Fallen angels with bad intentions
Tag teaming every robbery in the west
They were destined to be legends.

Lost souls catching midnight trains
Riding away with the wind
They'd steal your heart in a second
Then never be seen again.

She loved them both in different ways
They loved her, each in their own
Even after those many years and women later
She remained the only love they'd ever known.

They'd talk of her often next to the fire
In a new town late at night
Sharing the memories of the love she gave
Hoping one day they may reunite.

Dalisay

Tiny Fairies

Yes - it is true,
I once believed that I loved you.

Just as I once believed in fairies.

Dalisay

Dalliance

From the moment I saw you
I knew you would be the end of me -

And I would let you be.

Dalisay

Should Have Seen This Coming

We should have seen this coming, my love
But we decided to play hide and seek in this bed
Pulling the sheets over our eyes instead.

Gripping each other through the heat of the moment
Bitter Monday mornings when our eyes were
　forced to open.

Guilty pleasures and a wrong turn in judgment
Amidst the pillow-talk and screams
You became my weekend sacrament.

Lascivious

You told me that you're greedy
I replied,

You can take all of me
I am yours.

Ghost

I'm half asleep feeling your presence
Drifting towards you through your whisper
Somewhere in between my reality and my dreams
You seem to always linger.

Insulin

Magnetic
We needed each other

Electric
A passion I will never forget

Carrying on with your absence is hectic
But it turns out you're too sweet and I'm a diabetic.

His Promise

You're all I've ever known.

You're the sun on my skin in the winter morning
Your breath is my hope,
So, I inhale you – *deeply*

You're my solo smile in a nightmare
You communicate love to me through your fingertips
Smothering away my sins
Embracing me with your silk hair in the morning

I destroy everything I touch
And you grow flowers from the ash
I don't know how you do it
You're contagious and I caught you

I don't know how to do anything
Except love you -

In this life I have found you to love
And in the next I shall do the same.

Heartbreak

Tread cautiously

Vacancy

All I do is think of you
So I drown my mind in liquor
But you swam to the bottom to rescue me
And I woke up from it all even sicker.

I can't stand it, but I miss you
And I numb my heart in ways I shouldn't
Trying to fill this empty room you left in me
But I know it'll always be vacant.

More Than Words

She said she loved you
And your stare was empty
Your heart couldn't feel,
Your eyes couldn't see.

The love that she had
Was more than you deserved,
And yet she loved you
More than words.

Unlabeled File Cabinet

Shared experiences are what ties us together
  until the end of our lives
Somewhere you remain in the empty cracks of my mind.

Often walked over when in mid conversation
Once loving memories that now store
  as unimportant information.

Dalisay

I Don't Need You

But my soul does
She calls for you and I ignore her
Sometimes she screams for you so loud
  that I 'm forced to lock her away
I barricade her in a dark room next to your memory -

Because I can't stand to hear it
And I can't bear to believe it.

Remember My Name

You pushed me
Expecting me to fall
Silencing my voice with your screams
Ignoring my surrendering call.

You bent me
Expecting me to snap
Untwisting my brain within your fingertips
Letting the fragments rot in your lap.

You stabbed me
Expecting me to bleed
Over and over you left me resonating
Hoping that I would cede.

All of these terrible things you've done
All of the pain that I've endured
Karma will come back to find you
And when she does I am sure,
She will haunt you for a lifetime
She will avenge all of my pain
As you cower in panic at the sight of her
You will remember my name.

Dalisay

Cruel Thoughts

He said:
One day you will see.
You will soon live through
 all that you've done to me,
You soon will realize how deep my love was
And how no man in this universe
 can ever measure up.

I can't wait for that day my love,
I can't wait for that call
For that moment you confess
 when I left you lost it all -
For that instant gratification
I will feel through your pain
And I feel that day draw nearer,
 with each breath that you take.

Dalisay

Diabolical

I buried my heart in his hollow ground
Latched my soul to his sinister pneuma

He was the walking dead
And I was his conduit.

Dalisay

Grounded by You

We were passing souls who stopped for a minute
  to admire the other

Your eyes and mine fell in love
For those extraordinary seconds,
We were everything to each other

But the more we analyzed each other,
The faster we disconnected

*You were on another path
And I was from a different world.*

Leaving

Part of freeing him
Was leaving him;

And there was no easy way

There was only the inevitable outcome
  of breaking his heart -

Dalisay

Vs.

The worst part is that it happened
The best part is that it's over.

Don't Know Me Anymore

I'm fighting to stay a decent girl
And you're just fighting to keep me
I've torn myself to pieces up and down this house
Trying to remember who I used to be

You were reckless with my heart
I watched as our future gradually shattered
Just to keep myself sane from your havoc
I pretended my dreams never mattered

That girl who felt deep love is gone
But I want her back so desperately
Do you think that if I call for her
She will come back to me?

When she left, she stole my decency
And what little remained of my love
She left me as a used empty shell
Only to remember who I was

She left us here together,
Maybe she thought that I would just follow
Every day I sit here and pray
That she may come back for me tomorrow.

Surviving His Lies

I was once an innocent girl
Until this man came into my life
I fell in love with his charisma
And learned how to live a lie.

He taught me to deceive
And to always live in the moment
When he put his hands on me
The rest of the world became my opponent.

Dalisay

Your Message Has Been Sent

I sent you a message today
It reached an infinite abyss
Or maybe someone else
Or possibly no place at all.

But those words were meant for you
And even though you're gone
I can't accept the truth;
That you'll never respond.

Dalisay

Puzzle Piece

There it was. As real as I knew it was.

It existed in my mind and fed on my soul
I stared it in the face and felt somewhat whole

It was like finding the missing piece to a puzzle
That you've been working on for a year
And the more you tried to figure out
　how it all fits together
The more it felt unclear

But there she is, the missing piece
And I knew we both couldn't fit
I wish I could say I forgot that feeling
But it's easier to forgive than forget.

Goodbye Lonely

Even with all those women you possess
You're still the loneliest man I have ever known.

Dalisay

Inferno

There's a fire between us
I can see you through the flames
I hesitate to look away from you, fearing if I do
You'll shoot me down without restrain.

This barricading fire is also in your eyes
I can't escape its oppressive heat
I know you would throw me in it if you had the chance
I hear it in your voice as you stand before me.

This fire that once burned for other reasons
Now only exists to feed your soul
The same flames that we once shared to keep warm
Exists in my absence to keep you whole.

You choose to house this inferno
That incinerates our memories, the good with the bad
But I can't help but wonder what will become of you
When the fire burns out and all that's left is ash.

Onions & Men

I cried.

Not because you shattered my dreams
Or ripped my beating heart right out of me,

Not because you destroyed every hope I ever had
Or because you've showed me hate in ways I never knew -

I cried because as I chopped this onion
It forced me to cry.
That's just what onions do.

Kinda like you.

Numb

You were the realist thing I ever felt

And now after all the tears and pain
I am so glad that you're gone and I don't feel a thing.

Except, now I can't feel anything.

6.5

I don't wear that ring anymore,
But I kept it.

It reminds me of destructive youth,
Of broken promises
Believed lies
Sleepless nights
It's your ring of fights.

You may not understand
Why it sits in my dresser
Pushed around,
Sinking farther and farther to the bottom
Tossed aside -

But I will tell you why.

Because it's a symbol of what I was to you
And even though you prefer to forget that side of you -
I have chosen never to.

Home Invasion

You found a home inside of me
You buried yourself in my synapses without permission
And it was so cruel of you
To infest my brain,
To take over my life the way you have.

Slipping into Absence

You seem to be the only one that I can't stand
The only one I can't forget
I bang my head against the wall
Hoping the memory of you will fall out of it.

You seem the be the only one
That I just can't shake
I drown myself in tears and liquor
Until I finally numb this heartbreak.

But in my dreams, you remain
These feelings never subside
Every day I fight to neglect
This void you left behind.

In the Reserve

She spends every day under the cypress tree
Listening to the ocean in all its glory
The people passing in all their hurry
The birds singing in all their harmony

She spends every day beside the ocean
Wondering why she feels so broken
Wishing she could remain there, frozen
Silently wasting away,
Regretting the paths that were chosen

She spends hours upon hours dangling her feet off the cliff
Convincing herself that if she fell,
She would never be missed
Believing happiness is just a jump away,
A dive into the mist
For hours until sunset approaches
Then she is inclined to resist

Tomorrow shall be the same, I will watch her debate
Observing her from a distance, implicitly afraid
Admiring the same soul that she chooses to hate
I want to save her, yet I hesitate
We do this in silence, day after day.

Dalisay

Days in Counting

382 days and counting since I've last seen you
Not a day has gone by since then
That I don't incredibly miss you
Hardly a single breath of fresh air has been inhaled
Without even the slightest hint of you
And all I seem to do is drink more without you.

382 days checked off the calendar but I'm still waiting
Anticipating for the morning I wake up
And I'm no longer waiting
Waiting to let go, or for the day I stop wasting
Wasting these days away,
Erasing the images I keep repainting
Beautiful mural images all over my mind
And memories I can't stop retracing
Remembering our bitter night endings
Is better than this empty bed that I'm facing.

382 days have passed and I'm trying to let go
Clenching my fists toward my stomach and taking a blow
Pulling my hair out from the roots
Just to watch it re-grow
Facing the world smiling and screaming into my pillow
Going crazy and wishing I could go back to 382 days ago.

You Don't Love Me

He said, "I love you"
I said, "You don't love me"
He looked at me like I was crazy
I told him to show me
He put his hands on me
I said "exactly".

He said "I love you"
I said "You don't know me"
He smiled and said "You've told me"
I asked him what I was thinking
He put his hands on me
I said "exactly".

Dalisay

Knotted

He was a shadow, slick and empty
Full of greed and disparity
I push him away, but he was drawn to my purity
A complex chemistry,
He and I
He devoured me and I felt alive
I searched for his love for all my life
And yet, only did I find
Simply a Devil trapped inside.

Dalisay

Hollow

He looked at me
But did not see me
He could not feel me
He only saw what he wanted to see.

An object, a female
As if blood did not run through my veins
As if I cannot feel hurt or shame
Almost not worthy enough to have my own name.

Dénouement

To remain in your absence forever would have been an eternal tragedy

Dalisay

Tribute

One day you will no longer be here to read this
So it must be perfect now
It will never be finished
But it must be complete somehow

You must know that formulating the words to
  describe you
Is nearly impossible
And the love from our bond, although once was turbulent
Now stands strong and unbreakable

You have given me your best traits
I would be lying to say you possess anything but,
At 24 I have now just begun to understand your reasoning
I know now your logic behind the rut

There is a certain glimmer in your eyes
That I know I shall never find again
A special tone in your voice during our precious
  conversations
That reveals, I too am *your* best friend.

Old Soul

In this life she is untrusting
She says she is a "new soul"
Unhappy with everything she tries
She doesn't understand the ways of people.

My mother, she knows
That this is not yet her time
She is here now to get practice
For the day of her prime.

I am here to watch over her
She recognizes my "old soul"
More acceptable to human nature, I am
Therefore I remain more peaceful.

She will pass one day, but I do not fear
Because I know our paths will cross again
Whether it be 40 years from now or a thousand centuries
Our souls will forever remain friends.

Begging Tumble Weed

He walks with himself
He is his own best company
He pushes forward but you often do not notice
You ignore his plead as you perceive his struggle

A breathing tumble weed

Shrubbish, wobbly, and smeared,
He zig zags through the crowd

Sometimes he screams and he too cries
Sometimes he trembles in the night
Sometimes he dreams of better days

Just like you -

Dalisay

Don't Blink

Little girl with bright blonde hair
Cheeks painted pink
Playfully hid behind the table
Mommy do you see me?

Innocent eyes and a smile so grand
With a laugh so bubbly
She tested her mother, coming out of hiding
Mommy could you hear me?

Hide and seek,
She covered her eyes
Only just for a moment,
But she opened to a surprise -

Her baby girl had grown too fast
And she herself was aged and weary,
In the hospital bed she was fading fast
By her side her daughter sat,
Mommy, are you still with me?

Lioness

You fantasized about her
She was the lion that you could not control
She was the bright fire in the distance
That you craved to behold.

You wanted nothing and nobody above her
You extended your dark hands in her direction
You charmed her and tricked her
But I'm sure you have since learned your lesson,

You desired to cage nature's beauty
You stripped her voice and bound her ankles
You danced and raved "You're mine! You belong to me"!
Then you placed her in shackles.

Little did you know then,
As you starved her hunger
That she was the strongest of the pack
A natural born hunter.

You caged a Lioness
But don't you know you can't cage a soul?
She may have appeared as a weak one for a while
But you had never encountered one like her before.

Careless and shallow you were
You beat her until she broke
But all you did was bring out the killer in her
She broke through your chains and sliced your throat.

Analyzing the World

Sometimes she sits by the fire
In the middle of the night
She makes a small plate
And turns off the lights.

Sometimes she leans against her window
Staring out at the moon
Wishing on stars
Humming her favorite tune.

Sometimes you may see her
In her own little world
On a bus route somewhere
Gazing into the world.

She silently lives
But she's happy this way
Lonely as she appears, she is not
She is her favorite company - every day.

Dalisay

I Don't Drink

I don't drink
But when I do -
I lose myself.

And it takes a while to find me again
But then just as I find me,
I always drink again.

A Desert Dream

It was a seductive day in Phoenix
The only one I'd ever seen
Rain fell from the heavens so harshly
Turning this wasteland into an evergreen

Just as overbearing as the heat of day
This desert showed no mercy
The barriers were broken and the flood was released
Blessing this land with novelty

Thunder like drums through the midnight skies
Lightning to lead our way
For twenty-four hours, this place was pure ecstasy
Never was there a more enchanting day.

Little Feet

Little bare feet jumping from stairs, generating an echo
Running through the woods all day, snapping twigs
Relentlessly killing the life below.

Little bare feet that raced each other through these halls
She grew older and she grew wiser
Gaining strength from every fall.

Little girl, now not so little
Chasing new little feet
Through the house and out the door
Adapting to a new wild beat.

Monday's

I missed my exit this morning
My boss is blowing up my phone
I don't know what to say to her, my foot wouldn't let up
I continued south about three hours ago -

I'm not sure where I am or where I'm going
I picked up a few bad habits along the way
Somehow this tequila/coffee mix in my sparkle cup
Seemed like a good idea today.

These dusty roads have seen me before
The lost girls, numbing their brain through the stereo
I'll keep driving until I run out of gas
Or until I reach the border of Mexico.

- About -

My book is titled Dalisay, a name from the Philippines meaning 'pure'. Each poem I write is a genuine thought or feeling, each stemmed from a unique origin. For that reason, the meaning behind the word is most fitting. It was important to me to select a title that represents each individual poem and the collection as a whole, as the pure emotionally inspired creativity that they are.

I began writing when I was eight years old. What started as a simple interest in word play on notebook paper, transformed to become a freedom that I relied upon as an adolescent looking for an outlet to document my emotions.

Poetry for me today is more than just a creative hobby. It is the part of me that bridges the gap between beautiful and chaotic, and it sparks at any given moment. It only takes one thought or memory to trigger something full of imagery and rhythmic verses.

Whether I write about myself or a fictional character, there is equal sentiment in each piece. Although many of my writings are based on memories, not all are experiences that I can claim.

I look forward to sharing my next book with you.

Website: www.SonderRPublishing.com
        About Sonder R. Publications
        About The Author
        News
        Author's Blog
        Contact

Instagram: Sonder.RPoetry
Facebook: Sonder R. Publications

SRP

www.ingramcontent.com/pod-product-compliance
Lightning Source LLC
Chambersburg PA
CBHW022113040426
42450CB00006B/687